A Book Like This

BOOKS BY RAMA KABA

When It Comes to Love
When It Starts to Hurt

A Book Like This

poems

Rama Kaba

Zircon Press

A Book Like This

Copyright © 2024 by Rama Kaba

All rights reserved.
No part of this publication may be reproduced, distributed, or transmitted in any form or by any means, including copying, recording, or other electronic or mechanical methods, without the prior written permission of the publisher, except in the case of brief quotations embodied in critical reviews and certain other noncommercial uses permitted by copyright law.

For permission requests, email info@ramakaba.com
"Attention: Rights & Permissions."

ISBN 978-1-7382614-0-6 (paperback)
ISBN 978-1-7382614-2-0 (hardcover)
ISBN 978-1-7382614-1-3 (ebook)

Published by Zircon Press
Cover and Interior Designs by Alex Demanin
Cover images by Brandi Redd on Unsplash (open book)

www.ramakaba.com

Dear Reader,

This is not a traditional content warning note. There is no list of potential triggers in this book. However, since some of these poems were not so easy for me to write, I figured they may not be easy for you to read, so please take care. This book is meant to uplift and inspire. If you read a poem that brings painful memories or makes you uncomfortable, take the time to process it and keep going—just like in life.

Thank you

Contents

PRELUDE
A Book Like This   3

ONE
Where The World Began   9
Over Mount Nimba   11
Always Around   13
A Million Cessations   14
Legacy   15
Inheritance   17
Djeli   19
An African Woman   20
Young Dreamers   21
The Soundtrack of My Life   22

TWO
Made in America   25
The Colour of Black   27
Latchkey Kid   29
Washing Day   30
That Rainbow   31
A Choice   32
Billie   33
Voices   34
The Leaders of Music   36
Fly   39
An American Ethos   40
The One   42

THREE

Motel   47
Scars   48
Blues   50
Barren   51
The Loss of You   52
Moving On   53
Bullshit   55
A Price   57
The Only One   58
Empty Promises   59
Sharps   60
Trust   61

FOUR

End of Summer   65
Read Me!   67
Those Words   70
The Problem   72
Give Thanks   73
DWP   74
The Spectator   75
A Life Worth Living   77
A Job   79
This Girl I Used to Know   80
Beginning of Autumn   81

FIVE

A Woman 85
Knowing 86
The Yellow Lines 87
I am What I am 88
Families 90
A Welcoming Place 91
A Beauty 92
My Credence 93
Body Figure 94
Black Girls Do Cry 95
First Woman 97
Life Lessons 99

SIX

Omniscience 105
Alive 106
Deduction 107
Midnight Thoughts 108
Heal 109
How to Catch Yourself 111
A lady 112
Expectations 113
Empty Words 114
Flight 115
Thank You 116
The Shape of Black 118

PRELUDE

A BOOK LIKE THIS

It never comes easy
like the /s/
that always lingers
on the tip of my tongue.

I struggle
                                                                       to

                be
                                    in   this
moment.

A book like this
                                        needs you to
                                                 look
beyond your own—
to admit
to what you've always
shut out.

Please don't
continue to hold
only your gaze
when there are ways
to raise these letters
to be better.

A book like this
does not speak in tongues.

Words do not string
beyond their detonation to sting.

A book like this

                                          is not a theory.

Don't be leery

                    of words b

                              lee

                                        ding

      over

            margins.

Facts will not be cut off when bounded,
when you find differences
between fonts sizes and colours.

Let's appraise the ways
a book like this
captures those adjabs,
abugidas,
and syllabaries.

Decipher those pictograms
and logograms
and even ideograms—

because a book like this,
represents,
despite my continuous efforts,

to capture,
    to articulate

              my inability
              to express,

      my thoughts
  and feelings.

A Book
Like This

                is a
              book

        of my own.

『ONE』

WHERE THE WORLD BEGAN

i once lived between the Afr ca.
Its name, foreign lips
can never wrap their tongues around.
Its name resembles ripples of colours.

I once stood where the ocean ended,
and the sun extended its arms
to skeletal kids with big bellies,
who blended in with the darkness of the earth.

Where it was okay for virgins to give birth—
How else to explain bare feet
blackened with the ashes from death?
Or the muddied waters
that tasted like sugar beets?

I once lived where diamonds
were tucked under the Earth's soft breast,
and gold submerged in her distressed eyes.

Dressed in blood, she was carried by the Nile.
Her history stolen and filed under Third World.

I once loved where birds carried you;
where skin glistened in the morning sun,
but remained darker than the starless night.

Her lover's hand caresses her thighs
as she wonders if his loving and seed
would leave her dead under the cacao tree.

I once died where souls were sold for salt.
Where the White Sea took her children;
where you could touch the clouds;
hear the lions roar; and you knew, you knew,
no matter where you'd been taken
this was where the world began.

OVER MOUNT NIMBA

I walk barefoot;
I can't refuse
with soil so clean and rich
to support my plantar fascia.
Sideways, crescent shaped,
rivers are born here.

Over Mount Nimba,
I spend my childhood
scraping my knees,
and running shirtless;
the wind gracing my scalp—
I dust cocoa powder off my chest.

"I ni sooma"*
echoes over Mount Nimba,
as the morning sun
wavers from east to west.

Over Mount Nimba,
uncles break kola nuts;
eat Senegalese Jollof rice
and discuss the bride price.

A prize, I will never collect
in this patrilineal system.

But a family name,

---

*. Good morning in Maninka (Guinea and Ivory Coast).

I can easily trace on all sides
of Mount Nimba.

ALWAYS AROUND

I count all the stars
and come up short;
nothing compares
to your love and care.

You carry me
on your back
till I can wrap my legs
around your soft belly.

I sleep under your long breasts,
dreaming dreams
where you're always around—
I don't go hungry.

I don't miss
who isn't there.
I see them in your eyes;
I hear them in your voice.

I inhale the ethereal scent
of bergamot in your scarf
as I fly over the Atlantic—
because you're always around.

A MILLION CESSATIONS

A million cessations—
nights are no more.
Sun rises over
the cacao trees.
Sweet cocoa butter
scent wavers,
caressing my dark arms.
I glare at the moons,
wondering if
this is the other ending
grand-mère whispered
during my early days—
as my bare feet sink
into the red, red
dusty soil.

LEGACY

I wear my skin out
so I'm always cold
never do what I'm told.

I was born charred by the sun:
he wished I was his son.

He forgets
it is I
who will bore him this legacy.

Crooned past through the lips of djéli,*
I carry his name
beyond what he could afford,
a Pink Star encrusts in earth's breast.

Only I will be able to nourish and let him rest,
let free the king in his mind.

I carry this legacy:

      my children will be born with the night.

They will carry the strength of darkness
and emerge with the hope of light.

I bear this legacy:

---

*. French spelling of griot.

             it is an honour
to rise
and still rise;

             to live.

INHERITANCE

Daddy told me,
"This is it."
The blood that runs
down my thighs
once filled the Nile.

My children
will bear the marks
running down my spine
even if I choose to live
in denial.

Mama told me,
"You are strong."

The scars hidden
in my uterus
will not reveal itself
until I meet him.

I must bear him
in the eyes and confess
that my scars run so deep
that our children will
never taste his privilege.

They will not inherit
what he's never had to fight.
Instead, they will learn to fight
for wars that cease to end—

an equality, that's rightfully theirs
in countries that continue to live
in denial, that refuse reconciliation.

DJELI*

I always thought that I'd be a singer.
Those dreams—
I never got to feel their vibrations
before my vocal cords were snipped.

"You can't become a djeli."
Your forefathers have not done the work.
They have not sealed blood
to carry words over the centuries.

I've never witnessed my uncles fine tuning koras,
or tightly stretching drumheads over the djembes,
or contemplating whether to free
or fix the keys of their balafons.

My family name
won't afford me one.
I must shed this name
if I want to be heard over the mountains.

But I don't; instead, I find solace in silent songs—
written over crisp white sheet.
My eyes sing with a slow cadence
as my fingers graze these written words.

---

*. French spelling of griot.

AN AFRICAN WOMAN

Knowing I can climb
to the top of my family tree
has been the only thing
keeping me grounded.
When I feel sad,
I just remind myself
how lucky I am to know
where I've come from.
Tracing the lines in my hand
to a land called Mother,
I know where I've been,
and where I want to go.

YOUNG DREAMERS

I felt it slipping
when I was twelve
and thought I held
a fourth dimension.

I knew the meaning of time,
its rhythmic sequence:
sunrise and sunset;
night and day.

They say,
she went in peace—
but my heart hurts
with this ineffable feeling.

Qualia—in time,
we will experience
these inevitable events—
we are born; we die.

I felt it slipping,
when I was twelve
and realized this is how
it started—the unveiling.

THE SOUNDTRACK OF MY LIFE

Bambino's Kassa accompanies me abroad.
New land, familiar faces stare back at me.
As I suck in cold air for the first time,
and feel it sneaking under my bazin,*
I long for Folon— Keita's gritty voice
scratching my malleable spine.

Feeding the tape through the tape guide,
my pinky finger spins the take-up reel,
ensuring a tight fit.
No skipping as I take in looming skyscrapers.

When I can finally press play,
I need Sangaré's comforting voice
to start the soundtrack of my life—
the life, I want to live.

---

*. Bazin is a high quality African fabric made from cotton. Also known as a brocade dress.

『TWO』

MADE IN AMERICA

You've birthed me—
I was naked.
He entrapped me
in cotton and tobacco;
smoked my woolen hair.

I'm pushed into black soil—
nails cutting roots—
coloured me so dark,
the stars hid with coal.

I saw Her;
I followed her.
Drinkin' Gourd
twinkling in her eyes
as fireflies whisper
cunning lies.

I was unmarked—
you birth me;
entrapped in cotton,
but I unearth
soft, fluffy yearns
to find fields of chains—
ah, cotton is king.

No matter
how much smoke
fills my lungs,
choke my words,

I will sing
these stories.

THE COLOUR OF BLACK

The colour of Black
is a deep nebulous genesis;
no finite origin.
An absorption of sunlight,
warmth betided in its core.

A failure of semiotics
to understand the array
of perpetual momenta
as racist hermeneutic approaches
drove centuries of deconstructing Black.
Vilifying black. Exploiting black:

black sheep black magic blackhole black plague
black-hearted black mood blackmail blackface black boy
black girl black baby black child black mama black daddy
black mamba
blackie

Two sides: life and death.
No breath.
Yet, negative connotations catapult
generational genocides.
Black still rises—
still, the strongest in its neutrality.

Black   births   all   colours.

The colour of Black
is blood, an amaranthine will

continuously rising
after every attempt to strip it
down to a misconception
of white purity.

But such is the audacity of unchecked privilege—
How they forget—
refusing to believe
black swallows the light—
      that peace resides in the dark.

LATCHKEY KID

It's the afterschool special—
escaping to the library
until closing time.

My keys chime
as I drag my books home.
I've got a lot of playtimes
to roam before bedtime.

A book a day
keeps the Bloods
at bay.

WASHING DAY

This colour does not wash off.
Nah, it's not paint you can peel off
whenever you have a mind to.

Yeah, it smells as wild
as bird of paradise,
as cocoa and shea,
and sometimes, mango peels,
sweet hibiscus summer nights
sipping frizzy soda pop.

Fire hydrants uncapping
into joyful screaming mouths.
Pink tongues glazing out.
Black and brown bodies
cooling down.
That moment we ruled
167th Street & Walton Ave.

Nah, this colour
does not wash off.
But it can cool down
as it tries to shed
generational trauma.

THAT RAINBOW

race. europe bred it. america fed it. the ideology of colorblindness clouds the ability to see systematic oppression of others. colorblindness only works for colours that's never been contested. leaves you blind to other's diaspora. how can you account for and comfort systemic racism if you can't see where hues get darker?

seeing race doesn't make you racist. nah, this is the confirmation that race is a social construction. this is the consciousness of others' positions and perspectives. how can you be a part of the solution if you can't see the problem? how can you complete the equations if there's no bracket to separate ontology? acknowledging your own existence is not enough. finding your spot on the rainbow is not enough. you must also notice missing colours from that rainbow.

nah, merely seeing is not enough. you must be willing to stretch that rainbow and paint in those missing colours. it isn't enough. you must be willing to stop. stop black dead bodies. stop dead black bodies from floating as they try to etch in a spot on that rainbow.

A CHOICE

You say slavery is a choice—
only because you've never looked
yourself in the eyes to the truth
that marks the hues of your skin.
You may wash yourself hard,
bleaching product cascading down the drain,
but you will never erase the decades
of enslavement your mom's mommy's mother endured.

You say slavery is a choice—
can you face your dad's daddy's father
when the time comes?
Will you deny the generational pain
and the dreams of one day tasting retribution?

Freedom must taste like a half-ass smile.
You hide behind your beats, masks, and gloves.
Can you catch your breath though?
Or is your wealth compressing
your ability to remember your history?
A history I've only begun to decorticate,
peeling layers of forgotten truths.

You say slavery is a choice—
I wonder then if it was you enslaved,
if you would still hold firm to your belief:
slavery is a choice.

BILLIE

Don't tell me
this is a state
of the mind.
Tell it to the mama
whose boy swings
to-and-fro
like strange fruit.
Is it really 2021?
Yes, because blood in root
poisons seeds.

Sing it to me
the look
in the daughter's eyes—
a witness
to her daddy
washing up ashore.
Strange,
yet not so strange
to hear Billie's
rhythmic
swing song
echoing
even at the front
of the plane.

VOICES

Hey you!
Yes you!
You too black?   *Bleach yourself.*
Too pale?   *Tan yourself.*
Damn, you fat!   *Starve yourself.*
Wow, you did good girl—but wait—
are those your skinny bones poking holes in your clothes?

Cut yourself.
Stupid, stupid, stupid.
Just plain dumb. Drop out of school!
You're not a winner! Just keep losing.

Oh, I'm sorry, am I not nice?
Well, you should think twice
cuz you wouldn't cut a price.

Is this voice getting too heavy for you?
Am I crushing your breastbone?
Ha! Where are they anyways?
You must be missing a hormone or two,
Cuz you flat as pancakes!

Suck it in.   Hold it in.   Push it out.

These aren't internal dialogue—yet.

These are outside voices
and you've got choices!
Keep them out—

they don't belong.

Just keep pushing
until they can't get in.
Don't give anyone the power
to define you,
control you,
hurt you.

Don't let those voices ever settle...;
make a home in your mind.

THE LEADERS OF MUSIC

Why did the people stop singing?

Where are those saccharine smiles
that tasted just right
on the gliding diphthongs during recitation?
What about those eyes that kindled so bright
as the scintillating sun delighted in dark skins?

Where is the speech that used to preach
that it's a sin to bleach our skins?
Maybe we need to re-teach the truth
and pain about beauty being skin deep.

Why did the people stop dancing?
Where are those wobbling ashy knees
that marched for more than 300 days and nights?
And those nappy fros that swayed to the beat
of freedom and marked the knights?

And let's act like the segregations, the bombings,
and the KKKs were all right—
that the constitution didn't invite the exclusion
of race and gender as ways of evolution.

Why did the people stop listening?
To the contributions of X and King,
who united people into colourful revolutions.
Their attributions spin the world on its axis
prompting youth into selfless action.

Then why, oh why, are we enslaving ourselves
in today's institutions by remaining unconscious
to the eurocentric education we receive—
this is just another commission for retribution.

O.K.
Listen now, listen to the words
that I am about to sing;
so let your hips sway to the ways
our Sisters and Brothers used to play
till the night cited their long days
of carrying cotton.

Listen to their smooth voices
hollering over society's head,
to dance in the humid stilled air.
Thick like molasses,
their voices had a flow
that even the Southern bitterness couldn't breach.

Can you see how their slim callous hands played
the guitars?
Each chord feeling their blues
as their words indulge in doubletalk
for the shock listeners
who were never marked by the sun.

O.K.
Listen, listen now!
There's no excuse when you abuse views
that don't induce your views.
Your thoughts
are infused with reduced narrations.

Your incomplete translations are half-truths.

You never ask for explanations
when you receive diluted information
about human relations.
You got technologies that continue to ooze
ideologies;
such demands for cultural sovereignty.

You indulge in cultural imperialism
and misogynistic themes
toward the one who bore you,
all in the name of fighting oppression,
when really, it's just your accession
toward fame and money.

Don't say a word, just listen!
"I heard it through the grapevine"
that a change is coming…
"A change is gonna come,"
and we are all going to be alright,
even if I never met my motha.

Even if I never traced the lines on my fatha hand
to see if he would be a grandfatha.

Even if I never met Hughes and Holiday,
Medgar and Park,
I still sing and dance—I still have a dream.

FLY

My people could fly.*
Generated enough gravity to try.
Light framed and hollow bones—
but they were trapped down with stones.
Their wings nicked, snipped, snapped—
into the water, they adapted and learned to float.

---

*. Inspired by *The People Could Fly: American Black Folktales* by Virginia Hamilton. I was introduced to this folktale in the fifth grade, when I was still learning English, so I always dreaded reading it out loud. But I soaked in every word and spent that summer learning to read it all on my own. It was my introduction to African American history and has always stayed with me.

AN AMERICAN ETHOS

When I was young
I was told to dream
of lands across the Atlantic.
Lights always on,
Palladian and neoclassical buildings
built on the backs of blacks
as if they weren't dragged
like sacks of mulch.
Skyscrapers, steel frame
with curtain walls.
Smoothly paved roads
take me to schools
carrying books with half-truths.
Political pedagogy
continues to shut down
black and brown narratives.
Blinkered and inaccurate,
will it ever change—
where it matters the most?

When I was young
I was told to reach
for stars and stripes
waving in the air.
Even if it meant living
next to a house proudly
flying the Battle Flag.
You can stay blind,
but Southern heritage
is slave narratives.

There is no shame
knowing the wrongs
of yesterdays,
if it means you get to correct
the dreams of tomorrows.

When I was young
I was told to dream
of lands across the Atlantic.
Now, I yearn for the various
red,
yellow,
green
dancing in the air.

THE ONE

I don't mind being the one
to tell the world:
you've mistreated me.

Generations after generations;
centuries after centuries,
monotonous mistakes are repeated
because children become adults
nursing home-grown ideologies.
It's the foundation of modern relations.

Today's continuous ignorance is no surprise.
It's no mystery that
the collective African diaspora is still fiction—
an action thriller glamorized
because the view of mainstream media
is still filtered through a white gaze.

Don't be fooled;
empires were/are built on black backs.

I'm still stigmatized;
polarized, whenever my skin voice
its forced choice—
the inheritance of being black in the Americas.
The mortar used to bind America
is the blood and sweat and tears of slaves.
We must never forget
black lives are beset by the white knight,
especially when it seems alright.

Do you trust to have a peaceful
night in your home?
Or go out for Skittles?

So I have to be the one.

I feel its caress…
At times, I wonder if
it isn't just the distress in the atmosphere.
Modern racism is like a faint breeze,
if you sneeze, you may just miss it.

But I don't mind being the one
to forgive the future
that has yet to come.

                I carry hope like pocket change.
               Full of pennies that burn my palm
      as I arrange the ways change does happen.

                       Change must happen.

               How easy life must be, could be
             if I could exchange the ignorance
                 of today into yesterday.

         So no, I don't mind being the one
         to rewrite and recite the birthright
                     of my children.

                    We must be the one

to create something rightful
for my children.

Something good they can pass
generations to generations;
centuries to centuries,
without wanting to wish otherwise;
without wanting to erase
the colour that makes them so resilient.

This much is true:
loving black
is not for the faint of hearts;
being black
is not for the feeble-minded.

THREE

MOTEL

When I was sixteen on the brink of seventeen, I lived in a Motel. Two double beds and no doorbell. Loose comforter threads dangling over the edge, taunting me to pull. A pledge I wanted to break. But pull I did, and with every tug, the ache in my chest started to disappear. Until it reappeared. So, I kept pulling and pulling and pulling until I swallowed the last thread and bled.

When I was sixteen on the brink of seventeen, I lived in a Motel. Two double beds and no doorbell. I had a friend who thought I could grab her the moon. She saw me as a boon to her fragile life because my eyes shone like the sun and lips always curled up and my cheeks puffed out, forcing my eyes to crinkle. I've always wished she saw beyond the lies held tightly in my gripping eyes.

When I was sixteen on the brink of seventeen, I lived in a Motel. Two double beds and no doorbell. A cut here, a cut there, to ameliorate moments I never knew how to appreciate.

SCARS

I

A synonym for surviving.

Daring to stand
when I've been squeezed and poked
in places I've always thought to give free.

Every morsel I give feels like fire
burning the pit of my stomach.
Acidic ashes rumbling in my mouth—
I swallow this dire taste.
If I keep swallowing, will I drown?
With bile?

My mouth is sewn shut.
I recognize your mid-phalangeal hair
on the hand covering my lips and nose.
As I breathe through my eyes,
tears slip between your fingers—
a melting glacier bouncing off sharp edges
until I float
in a pool of lifelessness
even as my waning eyes
contradict my frantic pulses
as your hand slips down.

"Stay still. I love you."
You whisper.

Always these memories—

I don't need these scars
to fade
blending
into the shade.

II

Always these memories—

Trauma to my skin;
marking epochal stories
of never being heard.

Now, I look with glee
as your hands shake.
Your eyes never dare leering into mine,
as I recalled the assured words
you whispered to me
so many years ago—
as I pass you some plantains
off your best friend's dining table;
as your daughter sits next to me
and squeezes my hands.

BLUES

Cafard words drenched in beauty.
A symphony of melancholic duty.
Painful memories always on the verge,
I long for drops of myrtle spurge.

I've got the blues, blues, and blues.
Bruises hidden in styles for miles—
These are my rules for handling the blues:
drenched in black, head to toe,
would you know I was once a queen?

A lugubrious fate—
how do I keep waiting
to see over the rainbow?

Oh, I've got the blues, blues, and blues.

BARREN

Sun has gone missing.
Dark days; she remains barren—
seeds will not implant.

THE LOSS OF YOU

Nature says you
weren't meant to be.
But I still wonder,
what I could have done
differently
to give you
a better odd
of surviving.

MOVING ON

Worlds divided;
mind undecided.
Trying to reconcile
despair and hope
in a discombobulated
limbic system
is asking still if God exists.
You believe
or you don't.

Constantly, on my mind,
an oxymoronic fertile of losses
I wish to leave behind.
What ifs on looming replay
as I struggle to stay
in these poignant moments.
I struggle to dismantle
the tightness in my chest,
the distress in my breast
in the rare moments of joy
I just can't let go.

Days turn to weeks,
weeks to months,
the final trimester looming
so close I can feel the phantom
of the littlest hand grabbing my finger,
squeezing my heart
as my uterus contracts.
But still, fear bubbles

in the pit of my stomach
refusing to let go
of grief
so I can simply move on.

BULLSHIT

I'm okay.
I'm good.

I have my legs, my hands,
something to stand on.

My mind is strong.
I'm okay.

I'm loud.
I just need to find my voice.

I just need to find it—
tune it and make it my own.

I can see.
I can hear.

I can smell.
I can feel.

There's nothing
wrong with me.

I'm cute and coy
when I want to be.

I'm okay.
I'm good.

I'm strong—
can't you tell?

Don't I sound
fucking happy?

A PRICE

Crisp winter morning
meets spring stifling air.
These are warnings
I dare not spare
to just coincidence.

Despair in your hands,
will you not let me stand
next to you—keep you warm?

Pretending for a moment—
a storm isn't brewing—

that life is uncomplicated,
at times unfair;

that the night is not fast approaching,
and the morning yet to come,
will not bare this truth:

loving you
comes at a price.

A price
this time
I can't afford.

THE ONLY ONE

lie, lie, lie
i lie with legs barely open
legs unshaved with unicorn hair
you kiss i'm the only one
you miss because the dent of her
sucks me deeper into the mattress
the scent of unknown number Chanel
chokes me as you push between
my half-closed legs

like a valley,
i used to spread them wide
i was always ready for you
when you whisper
it's me; it's all me
i'm the one; i'm the only one
it meant everything

I gave everything

but it was a lie
you were a lie

you said her name
                    and left me in the flame

EMPTY PROMISES

You promised me
stars and moons;
instead, I'm cleaning
stardust from my room.

SHARPS

stop
this is how you wanna live?
stop
that look
that slinks, blinks,
clicks and chinks

drop dead—
is that what you really want?

your ashes
hate
leaving smudges

never let go
of grudges

otherwise,
what was the point?

TRUST

Decisions, decisions—
She was never good at making them.
Best intentions and a kind heart
don't stop vultures from tearing her apart.
It doesn't stop the raping of her mind—
her beliefs shredded into fine pieces.
Over time, people's faith in her starts to decline.
They retract and extract stacks of receipts
to recheck her words
as if she engages in gobbledygook.
Because decisions, decisions—
She never learned how to make good ones.
If only best intentions stopped crows
from eating what she didn't know.
Giving her the space and time
to learn from her mistakes—
to rebuild her reputation.
Decision, decisions—
actions have consequences.

FOUR

END OF SUMMER

It was almost the end
of summer,
and still,
you didn't pick me.

But I'll be bold and fold
my hesitations
and frustrations.

The shape of your lips
cast its own script
with me as the leading actor.

Your delay does not factor
this pheromone
that has me misbehaving
into a woman

who sleeps with wolves;
who runs with courage.

Even under the slithering heat
and uncertainty,
I will greet

your eyes with confidence
until the end
of this summer.

Whatever your decision,

come fall, I've got a hunger
not even the coming breeze
can cool into a sated satisfaction.

READ ME!

I heard what you said
             AND
saw what you didn't.

Read me!
Because I would rather die
a writer than live
knowing my words never scratched your tongue
into blistering recitation.

Your accusations:
SIGMA caused STISM—
Such complications
as my Si be ri an
silence creaks and cracks
hissing sibilant sounds.

Comment j'aime grésiller le S sounds
tu te moque de moi !

In prepositions, I live.

I know you hear those cracks
when my teeth ambush my phat tongue,
you /as/.

Oh my STISM in all its complications—
they were your foundations
for that tongue you sleep with teases me:

Zip.   Chip.   Sip.   Slip.   Strip.
Words, my mouth tests out
in shameful frustration.
In my father's tongue,
I mimic you live:
Sip. Zip. Sib.
But the vibration of your hungry tongue
swallows my /s/ /z/
/ʃ/ /tʃ/ /dʒ/ /ʒ/
usage for breakfast.

Read me.

My verbs teasingly slap and clap
against your alveolar.
I'll just stick to diphthongs
and monophthongs,
and let them glide on my tongue
as you keep your fricatives.

I can carve language.
Dare language into o b d ence

I can seduce it sloppy.

Slice it
and still make it gaga.

    I

        can

            slow

                it

                    down.

When those sibilant sounds betray me,

just read me!

Lis-moi !

Ne caran…[*]

---

[*]. Read me in Maninka (Guinea and Ivory Coast)

THOSE WORDS

i need the words
those times
action is merely a whisper
that feathers my spine

give me the words
fill it with pressure
i feel the symphonic vibration

the words are mine
and mine
to capture, to replay

when you pass time
i can still hear
the hemidemisemiquaver
of the words

never full
never meaningless
these words
are mine

give them to me
I'll chant them
over and over

and over and over
and over and over and over
and over and over and over and over

until i've created my own mnemonic
technique of never
regretting those words

please,
give me your word.

THE PROBLEM

no acknowledgement
of others' accomplishments
adds to the problem

you don't have to agree
to the same degree
to address and progress

the problem

check yourself to correct yourself
detect and reject
anything less than respect

suspect and inspect
the problem

to assess and amass
a solution

it's the only retribution
needed for a conclusion

to the
problem.

GIVE THANKS

Stolen lands—
dreams come true
for the victors.
Such arrogance
to lay claims and draw lines
to lands already inhabited.

Children of immigrants—
There's no excuse to misuse
the little fortune raining upon us.
As imbalanced and unequaled
it may be at times,
we must always give thanks
to those whose backs
were etched into the ground.

DWP

In classes, you were my first,
as if nothing else existed.
But I must confess,
your words did turn my head.
But I made the mistake
of letting my eyes
drift off your crafted words
into the lives you lived.
I should have known
to expect nothing
but disappointment from
Dead White Poets.

THE SPECTATOR

I see you.
Do you see me?

Draw your eyes
to my thighs,
breast
back down
to my hips and ass.

When I see you,
I know you.
When you see me,
you validate me.

Draw your eyes
to my hair.
Put me on a pedestal.
Look at me—
am I not all you
secretly desire?

The first time
I learn
I only exist
in your gaze,
I embody
first innocence.

Beside you,
I become a consumption,

feasting for the eyes
all so I can be
that artist.

A LIFE WORTH LIVING

Is this it?

All I have to show are series of events.

Unfortunate—
at times,
my breath catches
in my chest
as I rest my arms midair to feel…
Just to feel,
to be alive—
to live.

But is this it?
Am I okay,
if this is all there is to it?

A life—
I've been subjected
to live within predefined notion.

Constructed norms and customs,
some I cherish,
others I wonder
even as I shed those notions,
could I be reborn
into a life
I could ever call my own?

But is this it?

Sometimes,
as my head rests for the night,
and there are no lights
to expose the rupture
in old memories,
I find myself believing:
yes, this is
a life
worth living.

A JOB

It's crazy to think I've fallen trapped.
Bought into you—letting myself believe
what I was getting was okay.
It was not okay; it is not okay.

A cloud of distrust always lingered,
but remained out of my grasp.
It was easy not to chase
because I gave you my time—
nearly all my time.

I'm forgiving myself
for not realizing the entrapment,
the secrecy,
discrepancy—
that the falsehood of saccharine praises
was to keep me
trapped in this role,
to believe
any time now, I would advance.
Any time now,
I would be recognized.

But no more!
I now know
life is not a job.

THIS GIRL I USED TO KNOW

I used to know this girl.
Her smiles could rule the world.
Her hands always remained open
to miles of opportunities and possibilities.
Her laughter soothes earthquakes and hurricanes.

This girl, I used to know.
But that was another time, another place,
we shared the same warmth,
enveloped in fortune.
Now her eyes blight a marsh of nothingness,
eradicating in the same wan of nothingness.

We need to save this girl.
Prayers, won't you repeat
your palms and surahs and mantras?
She needs us; we need her
to be this girl I used to know.

This girl who knew saving one
meant saving the world.
We need her.

I need her.

BEGINNING OF AUTUMN

The sun is at its peak. There's hope for summer lovers as stillness fills the air. The rapid, frantic thuds of my heart echo louder than the black and white woodpecker twirling around the tree. As I walk along the path, the air warms, and the sun plays peak-a-boo with the remaining branches of proud trees. The sun's glare glisters on the once cool surface of playful green leaves. The movement of air carries secrets and muted cries only the trees seem to know, reminding me, a battle is brewing. A season's war, as the nippy breeze transports the leaves through the air, falling in a mindless, yet colourful death. Already, some of the trees—casualties of the season's battle—shamelessly bare their nudities. Their skinny limbs are ready to gleam with ice, while their nutty, sometimes fresh scents die a slow death. When the dog-walkers, the joggers, and the bystander step and crush the leaves like ashes, their crunching sounds reverberate like seashells brushing against one another. I know the end is near. It's a losing battle for summer. But for every end, there's a beginning. Fall has finally arrived. And, I've barely survived summer.

「FIVE」

A WOMAN

i am a woman
often subjected to changes—
don't stand in my way

KNOWING

if only
knowing I
was that simple

i am simply is
is to be I
who grows into
a woman—

a black woman

just cuz,

context always matters

THE YELLOW LINES

When the yellow lines on the road end, you can no longer defend driving without your lights. No marks to guide you during cold blistering nights. You fiddle and twiddle your fingers around the steering wheel, wishing you didn't feel the white lines on the road bleeding unto the cheap ass asphalt that never deals well with winter. You default on life, so you run through red lights—slowing down…, crossing solid lines, yet here you still are.

When the yellow lines on the road end, you can no longer fight what is yet to come. You must embrace what you've been keeping out of sight.

When the yellow lines on the road end, you must draw your own lines to survive.

I AM WHAT I AM

Dark skin with chocolate eyes,
I am the creation of n'na* and n'fa**.

Secretive hair that never relaxes,
I am the reincarnation of Malinke
with a swirl of Fulani.

Thick lips with full liner,
I am the voice that continues to upsurge.

My scars aged better than Birkin.
They are priceless memories
collected over years of running
with boys, over concrete, under bridges
in mushy soft dirt.

Lisp—my struggle is real.
But I've got things to say
and I refuse to be defined by my inability
to perfect a hissing sibilant phoneme
that bares no correlation
to my intellectual mental capability,
or to see beyond the facade of this world.

I am what I am;
A reincarnation of Malinke
with a swirl of Fulani—

---

*. My mother in Maninka (Guinea and Ivory Coast)
**. My father in Maninka (Guinea and Ivory Coast)

smeared across America,
residing in Canada.

FAMILIES

I started with eight
grandmothers.
Across the Atlantic,
the number dwindled down
conforming to the norm.
But with maturity
comes living in truth.
As I recall the joy
of my early youth,
in a house
that has never known silence,
with eight grandmothers
and two grandfathers—
I will be your only wife.

A WELCOMING PLACE

Imagine,
if you only sweat
in the throes of passion,
when birthing warriors,
healers and leaders.

Imagine,
if you didn't have to explain
the space
your hair invades—
a natural repellent
to keep predators
and instigators away.

Imagine,
if you weren't just born
to endure, to survive,
to live within the confines
of always being reminded
of your place.

But instead,
remember, a place
you can trace
to the beginning of time;
a place
where you are a queen.

A BEAUTY

When I was young,
I longed to strip
what midnight gave to me.
I wished to blend in
with the morning mist—
piece by piece,
my articles frazzle
into the fog.

I was made to feel
hapless with skin so dark,
a stagnant target marked
as last option.

God don't like ugly,
yet harsh words
still oscillate
around my onyx skin
time after time—
till I've come to accept
a beauty of my own.

MY CREDENCE

I balance confidence
in the tilt of my head,
in the crest of my upper lip
as it curves into a smile.

I wear sensuality
like the cashmere scarf
caressing my neck,
brushing the tips of my hair,
draping between the slopes
in my breasts.
Do you want to feel?
Let your gaze trace
the smooth lines of age.

I keep courage
in the turn of my wrist,
twist of an ankle,
in the arch of my calves—
I heel toe my way
into tomorrow,
decadently aging,
and bravely embracing
the unknown.

BODY FIGURE

I'm thick—full, all over.
Love handles, I'm obsessed with.
Going hungry is not a willing experience
I want in my repertoire.
It's degrading to the farmers
and the dark rich soil
and the soft and the hard rain.
It's belittling of every girl
who's never truly seen herself bare;
who's never learned how to smile
at her reflection and feel the weight of her breast.
Nah, I would never miss
the chance to lick my fingers and kiss it in the air.
I've got a full ass that shines like glass. Full breasts
that never rest, and leave indentation marks
in my restless neck, that needs to be massaged
at least twice a month. I've got full figures
that hug clothes like honey
without ever spending a dime.
Body figure comes and goes;
like trends, you've got to set
and love your own style.

BLACK GIRLS DO CRY

Your skin marks your kin.
Those inherited sins
mislead you to the underworld.
Melanocytes stripping;
melanin dripping;
leeching rich eumelanin;
melanosome bleaching.

The smell of fresh raw flesh
excites the Cerberus
into stopping your escape.
You do not belong in Hades.
The shades marring your skin
do not define your grade.

This is not your destination.
You will escape this inclination
that you are less
than to accept these affirmations:
you deserve adoration,
praises beyond this proclamation.

Your mind defines art.
Your deep eyes refine light,
natural like the soil that carries the seed
that never grows weed—
the beautiful flowers you constantly breed.
Always seek that black strength
that lies in endurance—
the ability to still, thrive,

to still, forgive,
to see possibilities
in darkness where beauty is as clear
as the stars that guided Truth.

In this life, we do not fear tears.
What our ancestors bared,
we should not have to—
for black girls do cry
tears of joy and triumph.

Freedom should always be a right,
premeditated since conception.

FIRST WOMAN

I am what I am.
You've made me
what I am.
Yet you tore me down
when I refused to bow
to your credence.

Don't feel sad
for my derelict.
Love is a languishing sentiment
I've absolved myself of,
and how free I feel.

So, their blood, I spill,
filling thousands
of rivers yet to flow—
thousands of wombs yet to grow
with seeds of tomorrow
I dance with sorrow.

You've made me bad,
but I'm not mad
that I've been replaced.
Yet, you still couldn't resist
having her bore
the Original Sin.

But such will be the lot
for my descendants
who become one

with the night.

I am what I am.
None have mistaken me
for innocent.
I never said that I was
more than I am.
Even when lost souls
reach out for me in darkness,
dying in my arms,
I feel nothing
because I am free.

I cannot be sorry
for who I am.
I will not be sorry
for I am,
what I was made to be.

LIFE LESSONS

i haven't always been honest
with myself.
The ability to stare
into my reflection
and see my pupils dilating
and the frequent nystagmus
is something I've avoided.

I've spent my teen years
perfecting fake smiles
that radiated for miles.

Because for me to have fears
is to ask the ocean
if she has any emotion
with her schizophrenic waves.

I've spent my twenties
slowly learning
how to control my laugh.

Half of me
always struggled
not to fill silence,
even peaceful silence
my conscious ceases to disturb—

Just one extra letter
takes me from being a god
to a being—uncomfortable.

I've spent my thirties
quickly glancing at myself

still fully clothed
but wondering if
this is all there is
to the life I am living—

the life I've sidestepped
to the ceaseless wonderings
as I'm still hungry for more.

I've spent my fifties
searching for my forties
because I've shamefully hid
from ever slowing down
letting someone poke and probe
my breast;
avoid the sun
and moving around too much.

I've spent my sixties
wishing I had retried
before the sun rose
so I could take the time
to smell the air
and feel the wind
grace my scalp.

Somewhere in my seventies,
I count my luck
as I stare at the ort
of my last meal—

I realize
self-reflection is a bitch.

But no life is well lived
without regrets,
without wishing
you could do it all again.

Another chance
to right wrongs;
another chance
to do better.

SIX

OMNISCIENCE

I belong to no human.
Born in my own sphere,
destiny will not steer
what I have yet to adhere.

I belong to no time.
Somewhere in my prime,
I've counted diamonds
resting in Earth's mantle.

I belong to no space.
No trace of a birthplace,
Still, I've drank clouds;
I'm high in the sky.

I belong to no name.
Even with foreknowledge,
I do not seek to tame
free will.

I am who I am.

ALIVE

that moment
your breath catches
you realize
you are
is to be
alive
somehow, some ways
you've made it
this far
you take
deep breaths
to keep going

DEDUCTION

The time I told you:
"You've hurt me."
You did not hear me;
you did not see me.
You've multiplied my pain,
added a permanent strain
to what we could have been.
I've since subtracted you
from my life.

MIDNIGHT THOUGHTS

I am you when the moon kisses the tip of the sun, and our youthful days seem never-ending as we run and hide in the wind heading for the ocean. Swaying between the crest and trough of the waves, its energy lures us to the edge of our graves. We dance in motion, propelling closer to sooth—this true archaic truth—this is it—this is our lives.

This obsidian sand runs between my toes; a vibe I feel even in my throes. I see you when your eyes sink and your lips curl and your nose fades and your hairs dance with the wind, weathered, but still breaking down volcanic glass into black sand. The salty breeze droplets sitting on the tip of my tongue solidify into pink crystals—a blend of rarity. This is it—this is our lives.

With this remaining time, you'll never have to admit the imperfection embedded in the crooks of your arms. The tilt of your head, just a little too much to the left when you use doublespeak. The drop of your tongue and that clicking sound you make and the purse of your lips when you get caught. This sooth—this true archaic truth—I know you know…

I love you. So, will you let me keep loving you for times yet to come?

HEAL

I can heal from this avulsion.
Always felt a compulsion
to ensure my life with you
did not define all of me.
You are not the glue
that will patch these wounds,
nor could I see it be true—
even if you gave me a clue
to ask you to be only mine.

These unshared parts,
I selfishly kept away
because I was smart
enough not to display
the work I was doing to build
confidence and resilience.

As all things with you,
it was only a matter
of when your true self
would bare its teeth
to sharply cut my breath
and swallow me whole—
no traces of who I am;
the woman
I will always be.

In a trance of those few releases
I found underneath you,
on top of you, beside you—

you do not own me.
Those pleasurable moments
cannot measure and seal
the I that is me
because I walked to you alone;
I can walk out the door on my own.

And when our goodbyes are done,
I will continue feeling my way in life.
I am not afraid to dine and wine
myself into the cold nights
and let my hands explore
all of me as my mind wonders anew.

This much is true:
I can heal from a broken heart.
I must, if only to live again
to feel every second,
until a whisper in my ears
sends shivers down my spine,
as I give love another chance.

HOW TO CATCH YOURSELF

Have courage
to withstand the storm.

Have strength
to reform the norm.

Have hope to cope
with the slopes in time,

so that when you feel the slip,
you can catch yourself, always.

A LADY

I am a lady.
Not always quite true;
not always so proper.
Respect, I still demand.

EXPECTATIONS

What I have
is what I've been given
to live within my means.
I count my blessings.

I can't shoulder these expectations
that I must live outside my means
to support those who use golden spoons
to crack their morning eggs.

I will not crumble
under the guilt
in your eyes,
in your voice,

as you wish I did more
to those who can afford
to sit reclined with their feet up.
Yes, I sleep just fine at night.

What I have
is what I've worked for;
long days and longer nights,
I will only give without breaking.

EMPTY WORDS

It's easy to say words
the way leaves grow on trees.
To believe, you must stress
every syllable until you've extracted
all the phonemes and your tongue
collides seamlessly with your thoughts.

The bare trees resemble your actions.
In the middle of winter
your promises freeze in the air—

I like that;
I don't need empty promises from you.

FLIGHT

Even when you learn to fly,
the past continues to matter.
Your home in the sky;
fears begin to shatter
your space in the clouds.
Before you dare to fly,
make sure you've aired
past grievances that will
otherwise weigh you down.

THANK YOU

I want to thank you

for touching my soul.
Laughing with me—
at times, laughing at me.

Kissing my heart.
Believing in me.
Sometimes, doubting me.

Caressing my essence.
Cherishing me.
At times, forgetting me.

Caring about my dreams.
Listening to me.
Often, not trusting me.

Loving me,
for wanting the best for me
and giving me your heart.

I want to thank you
for being you,
without the ups and downs,

where would we find room to grow?
To be better and to love more?
I hope that someday we do touch the sky.

Thank you for the love
we both want to have in each other—
a mate, for now and forever.

THE SHAPE OF BLACK

An umbra—
complete absorption of light.
An equal pull luring in energy
of discombobulated figures
stretching into penumbra.
Moving beyond kinesthesia
to a mélange of synesthesia:
names are colours;
shapes are music;
harmonic array of emotions
constantly morphing into the other.
Through a gestalt lens—
the mind assaults the eyes,
forcing the shadows to meet,
to emerge a solid figure,
to make meaning
of this nothingness
because we cannot simply be
without epistemic notions.
We cannot simply just be.
Our eyes must always
categorize and classify
nothing into something.
We cannot simply just be.

Acknowledgments

A Book Like This holds a special place in my heart as it contains poems spanning over two decades. I owe a great deal of thanks to my friends and spouse for their support in bringing this book to life.

A special thank you to my three besties, Raquel, Joy, and Fareh, for listening to me read my poems and giving me invaluable feedback over the years. Raquel, you were always "willing" to be our audience, as Fareh and I took turns reading poems, from the middle of the road to sitting on the bench in the dark overlooking the water. Joy, thanks for always being a captive audience.

I want to thank Fay for her wisdom and for helping me organize this book. I also want to thank Carina and Peter for their masterful review and proofreading skills.

And finally, to my wonderful husband, Alex, thank you for always supporting my creative outlets and for helping me turn my visions into reality.

About The Title

In 2009, I heard Angus and Julia Stone, singer-songwriter duo (brother and sister) from Australia and fell in love. I can't recall how I stumbled upon them, but I'm sure it had something to do with searching for indie and folk music at the time. *A Book Like This* was their first studio album. Even though their first album isn't my favourite, I still really liked the title, so much so that it became the title of a poem I was writing at the time. Little did I know that several years later, it would become the perfect title for my third collection of poems. Though my book by the same title is vastly different on every level, this just shows that you never know what or who will inspire you if you listen to something different and stay open to new things.

Rama Kaba is the author of two books of poetry, *When It Comes to Love* and *When It Starts to Hurt*. She was born in West Africa but grew up in the United States. She obtained her Bachelor of Arts from York University and her Master of Information from the University of Toronto to become a very non-traditional librarian. She lives in Ontario, Canada.

If you would like to hear about Rama's upcoming projects, visit her at www.ramakaba.com.

www.ingramcontent.com/pod-product-compliance
Lightning Source LLC
Chambersburg PA
CBHW022042160426
43209CB00002B/37